STAR WARS

THE

JEDI MIND

Secrets from the Force for Balance and Peace

Date: 12/22/21

STAR WARS

THE

JEDI MIND

Secrets from the Force for Balance and Peace

Written by
AMY RATCLIFFE

Illustrations by
CHRISTINA CHUNG

CHRONICLE BOOKS
SAN FRANCISCO

Library of Congress Cataloging-in-Publication Data.

Names: Ratcliffe, Amy, author.
Title: Star Wars, the Jedi mind : secrets from the Force for balance and
  peace / written by Amy Ratcliffe ; illustrations by Christina Chung.
Description: San Francisco : Chronicle Books, [2020]
Identifiers: LCCN 2020025094 | ISBN 9781797205939 (hardcover)
Subjects: LCSH: Mindfulness (Psychology) | Peace of mind. | Jedi
  (Fictitious characters) | Star Wars films–Psychological aspects.
Classification: LCC BF637.M56 R38 2020 | DDC 158.1/3–dc23
LC record available at https://lccn.loc.gov/2020025094

Manufactured in China.

Design by Kim Di Santo and Evelyn Furuta.
Illustrations by Christina Chung.

10 9 8 7 6 5 4

Chronicle books and gifts are available at special quantity discounts to corporations, professional associations,
literacy programs, and other organizations. For details and discount information, please contact our premiums
department at corporatesales@chroniclebooks.com or at 1-800-759-0190.

Chronicle Books LLC
680 Second Street
San Francisco, California 94107
www.chroniclebooks.com

www.starwars.com

TO THOSE SEARCHING FOR CALM AND QUIET.

INTRODUCTION

THE JEDI CODE

There is no emotion, there is peace.
There is no ignorance, there is knowledge.
There is no passion, there is serenity.
There is no chaos, there is harmony.
There is no death, there is the Force.

The code that all Jedi strive to follow offers principles for being at peace and learning. In fact, these tenets are useful not just in a galaxy far, far away, but here in our own world. They resonate quite remarkably with mindfulness, the practice of being fully present and aware of what we are doing, while trying not to be overly reactive to external factors. Mindfulness is rooted in calm, quiet health, reflection, and balance to bring the mind and body into sync. It reduces stress and anxiety, and its practices are meant to help people tune in to the world, surrounding us with clear consciousness. The more we are actively in the here and now, the more we can teach our minds to recognize emotions and thoughts without getting caught up in them.

I'm a worrier. I dwell on the past, and I cannot stop wondering about the future. New situations make me anxious. Basically, I have a lot in common with C-3PO. When Leia instructed him to wipe the nervous expression off his face in *The Last Jedi*, I felt it in my bones. I try to manage my anxious tendencies, and I've found success using mindfulness practices—particularly meditation.

When I meditate, I think about the Jedi. My mind is always ready to jump to *Star Wars*, it's true, but it's a natural leap to connect mindfulness with how Jedi strive to conduct themselves. The image of Qui-Gon Jinn taking an opportunity to drop to his knees and center himself in the middle of a lightsaber battle with Darth Maul is etched in my mind. He appears to be taking the few beats he can to focus on the present; doing so hones awareness and how we react to external factors.

While the Force isn't present in our galaxy, we can still learn from how the Jedi use it to guide their lives. And we can use these lessons about the Force as a gateway to studying mindfulness and putting practices into action. My hope is that as you read (feel free to skip around or read cover-to-cover), you will find activities that resonate with you and get you to slow down, learn, and appreciate the moment, as the moment is unfolding.

THINGS TO KNOW ABOUT MINDFULNESS

- Mindfulness encompasses so much more than only meditation—so if meditation isn't for you, don't worry. Meditation is only one way to practice mindfulness.

- Mindfulness is accessible. You don't need to acquire any special equipment or go to classes. You can, for instance, take a yoga class, but all you need to practice mindfulness is an open mind.

- You can devote whatever amount of time you want to practicing mindfulness. It's easy to incorporate practices into your day-to-day activities, such as while waiting for coffee or taking a walk. Choose to make something you're already doing mindful, and if you continue to prioritize this, mindfulness will become a habit.

STARTING OVER

"You must unlearn what you have learned."

—YODA

PRACTICE:
LETTING GO OF SHOULD

· Notice the next time you use the word "should" (whether you think or say it).

· Question the source of the should. Why do you believe something *should* be a certain way? Why do you think you should or shouldn't have done something or behaved in a certain way? What can or can't be done to change it?

· Make a regular practice of observing when you use "should." Investigating why you use it will help you be more susceptible to learning, rather than being stuck in old ways of thinking.

Luke has many preconceived ideas about how the galaxy works by the time he arrives on Dagobah. Yoda repeatedly advises Luke to clear his mind and trust the Force. It doesn't really click for Luke until he sees the "impossible"—Yoda lifting Luke's X-wing from the swamp—with his own eyes.

Minds constantly measure everything against how we think things should be. But what is our source of this condition of "should"? Why that and not something else? Having preconceived ideas can block us from absorbing new information.

RELEASE

"Remember, a Jedi can feel the Force flowing through him."

—OBI-WAN KENOBI

PRACTICE:
THREE-MINUTE STRETCH

· Once an hour, stop what you're doing and stretch for three minutes. Set a reminder if you think you'll forget. The specifics of the stretch are less important than the practice itself.

· For a standing stretch, try standing with your feet shoulder-width apart. Slightly bend your knees. Lift your left arm above your head in an arc toward the right. Hold for thirty seconds and repeat with your right arm.

· For a floor stretch, begin by kneeling with your back straight. Lift your arms up and bend forward until your forehead and the palms of your hands are on the floor. Hold for thirty seconds and return to your original position for thirty seconds. Repeat.

While training Luke in the ways of the Force and the lightsaber on the *Millennium Falcon*, Obi-Wan shares this fundamental observation on the connection between the Force and the Jedi. As it guides them, it is also something like having an open channel of communication with the body and the living world.

We can feel conscious of the flow of energy and tension within our bodies by giving ourselves a break to gently stretch weary muscles.

TURN OFF AUTOPILOT

"Our actions are a reflection of our purpose."

—QUI-GON JINN

Ever a source of practical lessons, Qui-Gon's observation here shows an understanding of how intent informs behavior, as the two are closely intertwined. Investigating this connection in yourself can help you dig out of a rut.

One reason we may feel that we're going through the motions without actually recognizing them is because we're on autopilot. If the only reason for driving in a certain direction, or holding a certain belief is because we've always done so, it's an occasion to pause and break the repetition. Mindfulness can lend a hand in grasping the purpose of our actions.

PRACTICE:
ROUTINE DISRUPTION

- Routines are familiar and comforting, and knowing them so well may make tasks quicker. But shaking them up can be a positive refresh. Start with something small, such as changing the way you travel. Try new routes or new modes of transportation. Walk on different sidewalks, free of distracting devices.

- Alter this or any routine once a day for five consecutive days. At the end of each day, reflect on the newness of your experience.

IMPORTANCE IN EVERYTHING

"The Force is not a power you have. It's not about lifting rocks. It's the energy between all things. The tension, the balance that binds the universe together."

—LUKE SKYWALKER

Rey knows little about the Force when she comes to Luke on Ahch-To for instruction. Luke teaches her about the high concepts of the Force, and how they do not belong only to the Jedi. Easy to understand in theory, but in practice . . .

Mindfulness, like the Force, is not about lifting rocks—in our case the rocks we are trying to lift might be our personal or professional endeavors. It can be easy to mistake this part for the whole, which is that mindfulness is about a greater sense of attention than any specific application. By giving an activity all our attention, and immersing ourselves in a task, we can remind ourselves of this. Hone this mode of thinking by starting small.

PRACTICE:
MINDFUL IMMERSION

- Choose one of your least favorite or mundane chores—for instance, washing dishes, or even literally lifting rocks.

- Next time you need to do this chore, do it very deliberately. Let go of everything else except for the task, and wholly engage in it. Pay attention to each step and action. Use your senses; notice any sensations your body has while you work. Perhaps you'll discover something unexpected, even enjoyable, about a routine chore.

FREEDOM

"You don't have to carry a sword to be powerful."

—AHSOKA TANO

PRACTICE:
SCREEN BREAK

- Block off one hour a day to put away all screens, including phones, laptops, and TVs.
- Cook a meal, read a book or comic, play a board game—pursue any venture that doesn't require a screen.
- Increase the amount of screen-free time on weekends or days off, if possible.

The Jedi are guardians of peace as well as warriors who wield lightsabers, and they know how to fight with them when necessary. The weapon is important to them, but as Ahsoka observes, a Jedi's power does not derive from their weapon.

We don't carry laser swords, but we do carry devices that can seem as though they powerfully direct our lives. It might not always feel like it, but it's definitely possible to set aside our smart phones and other devices. They can be incredibly useful—even, in some cases, for mindfulness practice— but they also regularly become distractions, pinging and flashing and otherwise pulling our awareness away from whatever we are doing.

PURPOSE

"Try to remember, always put purpose ahead of your feelings."

—ANAKIN SKYWALKER

The Jedi Code holds that peace comes with an absence of emotion, recognizing that rash feelings and extreme emotions can lead to the dark side. Anakin shares a variation on this tenet with Ahsoka, advising that she approach planning a battle with intent rather than with heated emotion. A cooler approach can facilitate her best decision making.

Ideally, our days or weeks do not involve planning battles—though it may sometimes feel that way. But whatever we may anticipate needing to tackle, it can be useful to do so with clear intention. Different from affirmations or goals, intentions are about what we *want* to feel. Imagine them as signs guiding you to where you want to be.

PRACTICE:
SET INTENTIONS

· When setting a goal at the beginning of the day or week, also set an intention. Write it down. Intentions have no limits, so do not be afraid to be ambitious. Choose intentions that align with your values—for example: "May I feel open to new opportunities."

· Don't attach expectations to your intentions. Embrace them as attitudes you want to embody.

· Decide intention before meditation, as it's especially helpful in guiding your thoughts and actions.

LOOK UP

"Don't tell me what things look like. Tell me what they are."

—LEIA ORGANA

PRACTICE:
SENSORY EXERCISE

· Sit in a comfortable, upright position with your feet flat on the ground. Breathe naturally.

· Notice five things you can see. Take the time to look at the entire environment in your range of vision.

· Notice four things you can hear, particularly in the background.

· Notice three things you can feel. Maybe it's the floor beneath your feet or how your clothes feel on your skin.

· Notice two things you can smell.

· Lastly, notice one thing you can taste, maybe your drink at hand or your midmorning snack.

As the leader of the Resistance, Leia must be practical. She must know the facts, the truth of the situation at hand, to be able to weigh risk and make effective decisions as part of her responsibility to those around her. She seeks to know what reality is, even (or especially) if it is not ideal.

The way we want things to be does not necessarily line up with the way they are. To pull ourselves into reality and locate our minds in this point in time, we can use setting, reaching out with our senses to ground ourselves. This exercise is especially useful if you're feeling overwhelmed.

DO. OR DO NOT.

THERE IS NO TRY.

—YODA

LOVE YOURSELF

"Already know you that which you need."

—YODA

When Luke travels to Dagobah to visit Yoda for a second time, the ancient Jedi Master is on his death bed. He reassures Luke that his training is complete, and that Luke, somewhere inside, knows what he needs. Luke has doubts, but what Yoda says is true.

We tend to know for ourselves what we need to be at peace. Self-care and mindfulness go hand-in-hand. If we notice what actions satisfy our physical, mental, and emotional needs, we can develop a sort of repertoire, go-to practices to have handy for whenever we might need them.

PRACTICE:
AN ACT OF SELF-CARE

· Reflect on something you need to do to take care of yourself—possibly setting boundaries by saying no to a project, or going to bed early. Taking a nap, or a bath, or a walk, eat a good breakfast—anything you know will make you feel healthy and rejuvenate your spirits.

· Plan the activity not as an indulgence, but as a necessity. Block time on your calendar and treat it like an appointment you can't miss.

· Repeat as often as needed.

LET GO

"Always remember, your focus determines your reality."

—QUI-GON JINN

As Qui-Gon mentors a young Anakin, he imparts wisdom about being mindful. He explains the values of quieting one's mind. Maybe most importantly, he reminds Anakin that whatever he chooses to focus on will play a role in how his life unfolds.

Some circumstances are out of our control. But focusing on our current action is something we *can* control, and it can provide a sense of calm and capability. Our minds will wander; it is our nature. Sometimes our minds swirl with negative thoughts and worries. We can move these along by recognizing them for what they are, and not giving them undue weight. The more one practices observing unnecessary thoughts and not fixating on them, the easier this becomes.

PRACTICE:
THOUGHT OBSERVATION

- Find a comfortable sitting position and close your eyes. Center yourself by focusing on your breathing. In and out. In and out.

- Acknowledge any thoughts that wander into your mind while you're focusing on your breath, and let them pass. Imagine them as leaves flowing down a river. You do not need to stop to take a second look or get caught up in these thoughts. Remain in focus, and let them go by.

READ BETWEEN THE LINES

"One thing you may be absolutely sure of—if an item does not appear in our records, it does not exist!"

—JOCASTA NU

PRACTICE:
MINDFUL READING

· Choose a book and carve out some free time. Read.

· Bring your attention to your breath, and carefully read a single page. Take notice of any words or phrases that jump out at you or evoke emotions. What images, if any, pass through your mind? Question any words you don't know; don't skim over them.

· Repeat this for the next few pages, and then continue reading slowly, listening attentively to your own responses.

As the Chief Librarian of the Jedi Archives, Jocasta Nu has absolute faith in the records and holobooks in her care. If the information isn't present in those records, she believes it cannot be true. It turns out that she's wrong about this, but her conviction that books hold truths is valuable.

While there may be truths found in books, there are also truths that we bring to the act of reading that we can uncover. When we enjoy reading and getting lost in a book, we're practicing a form of mindfulness—focusing on the moment as presented, de-emphasizing the weight of our own thoughts, and losing track of time. There's another approach to reading that can be mindful in another way, through a different kind of concentration and awareness, as shown in this practice.

GROUNDING

"The Force is what gives a Jedi his power. It's an energy field created by all living things. It surrounds us and penetrates us. It binds the galaxy together."

—OBI-WAN KENOBI

Obi-Wan offers this definition of the Force to Luke in their first encounter. It's a lot for a farm boy to fathom, but Luke senses there may be much to learn from the former Jedi Master. Yoda later emphasizes this lesson on Dagobah, telling Luke the Force is "Here, between you, me, the tree, the rock, everywhere."

Contact with nature is an immediate reminder of the connection living things have to their surroundings. Even brief contact can serve as a welcome and centering reminder. Forest bathing (see page 46) is one option for communing with nature, but if short on time, try this practice.

PRACTICE:
NATURE LINK

· Go outdoors to a grassy area.

· Take off your shoes and socks and walk barefoot for a few minutes. Curl your toes into the ground.

· Notice how the dirt feels between your toes, and what the blades of grass feel like as they brush against your feet. Appreciate this connection between living things.

MOTIVATION

"I'm one with the Force. The Force is with me."

—CHIRRUT ÎMWE

A member of the Guardians of the Whills, Chirrut uses his knowledge of the Force to sharpen his mind and body. He does not have Force abilities, but he has belief. In times of duress, he voices this affirmation, bringing clarity and conviction to his actions. Chirrut utilizes the phrase as a sort of mantra to push himself to keep going.

Affirmations are a valuable tool to encourage positive thinking. They provide inspiration, and counteract the negative and often incorrect things we might think about ourselves. Over time, and through repetition, the subconscious accepts the repeated affirmations as part of our identities.

PRACTICE:
AFFIRMATIONS

- Define one goal you want to achieve. It can be about happiness, health, success, peace of mind, or anything you want.
- Write a positive affirmation in the present tense that supports this goal. For example: "I am compassionate toward others." Avoid negative or conditional words such as "don't," "can't," or "might." Write the affirmation as if it is something you are doing in this moment.
- Consciously repeat the affirmation every day. It's okay if at first you see yourself falling short of the affirmation. Stick with it.

TAKE A MOMENT

"Breathe. Just breathe."

—LUKE SKYWALKER

PRACTICE:
TRIANGLE BREATHING

· Picture a triangle in your mind.

· Inhale through your nose for four counts as you imagine tracing the first side of the triangle. Hold your breath for four counts as you trace the second side. Exhale through your mouth for four counts as you trace the third side. Repeat three times.

Luke helps Rey define the Force within and around her by having her sit quietly, close her eyes, and reach out with her feelings—while mindfully breathing. It is the first lesson he teaches her about the Jedi. Through these actions, and her connection to the energy field, she gains insight into how the balance of the Force works.

Mindful breathing can help us concentrate and center ourselves in moments of emotional distraction or turmoil. Taking a moment for a few deep, calming, oxygenating breaths can be especially useful before situations that may be stressful or benefit from clear focus.

FRIENDSHIP

"Be with me."

—REY SKYWALKER

Rey searches for her place in the galaxy for a long time and begins to follow the path to her true destiny when the Force awakens within her. She also recognizes that her place is within a community, and when Rey asks for support from the Jedi of the past, she utters, "Be with me."

Relationships can sustain us, and paying attention to them makes them still more rewarding. Attentiveness is something we can practice any time we speak to someone else. Our brains run in the background regardless of what we're doing—even while enjoying the company of a friend. But we can quiet the chatter. Active listening helps the mind stay in the present.

PRACTICE:
ACTIVE LISTENING

- Next time you share coffee or a meal with a friend, put away your devices and give your friend your undivided attention.

- Don't interrupt or look for opportunities to chime in with your own observations. Focus on what they are saying, what thoughts and feelings they are expressing, and soak it in. Wait until they have finished speaking to ask questions or make comments.

- Focus on your friend in the conversation, not on what you are thinking about what they're saying.

FOR DIFFICULT CHOICES

"This is a new day, a new beginning."

—AHSOKA TANO

Ahsoka supports the rebel movement against the Empire by operating as the secret agent known as Fulcrum. No longer a Jedi, she focuses her intention and efforts on assisting others in the struggle to bring more light and hope to the galaxy in a different way.

Every day brings the opportunity to make different choices. Whether we want to make better decisions for the planet or simply meditate more, the day begins with a choice and an action. Treat each morning as a new beginning. We must open ourselves to change, because change will always happen. Be ready to face any challenging moments in your day by drawing energizing oxygen into your body and brain.

PRACTICE:
ENERGIZING BREATHING

- Stand and slightly bend your knees. Bend forward from the waist, arms hanging loose.
- Take a long, deep breath and slowly come to an upright position, lifting your head last. Hold your breath for four counts in this position.
- Exhale slowly as you bend forward from the waist.
- Repeat five times.

IN THE HEART

OF THE JEDI LIES

HER STRENGTH.

—KANAN JARRUS

COMPASSION AND KINDNESS

"For every action we undertake, for every word we speak, for every life we touch—it matters."

—QUI-GON JINN

A paragon of patience and compassion, Qui-Gon extends an understanding and a cooperative spirit to everyone he meets. He understands the value inherent in all life. Qui-Gon exhibits this kindness with Jar Jar Binks, working with him despite the reservations other Gungans have about Jar Jar. It's this openness and faith in the value of others that also leads to a critical alliance between the Gungans and Naboo.

We can apply Qui-Gon's attitude to our interactions with ourselves and others. Even the briefest exchange can have an impact on someone. By purposefully practicing kindness, in seeking opportunities to be kind, we can also make ourselves more mindfully able to notice, and drop, habits of negative reaction we may have formed.

PRACTICE:
INTENTIONAL ACT OF KINDNESS

- Take a moment when you are near another person to offer a kind word, or to do something kind. It might be asking how someone is doing, sincerely listening, and offering encouragement. Or it could be opening a door. Even small actions can have a larger effect.
- Notice what happens, and how you feel, after your act of kindness.
- Offer kindness to others and yourself regularly, and you will be more likely to respond with kindness and compassion.

INNER VOICE

"Stretch out with your feelings."

—OBI-WAN KENOBI

When you can't see something clearly with your eyes, you can reach out in other ways to understand your surroundings. Obi-Wan imparts this knowledge to Luke in an early lesson about tapping into the Force.

A continuously running internal monologue tends to follow all of us, wherever we go, no matter what we are doing. Silencing the mind is near impossible, but observing our inner voice helps redirect it, no Force necessary. Close your eyes, but gaze inward and listen, without judgment. Giving our inner voice all our consideration means that, in time, we will come to know it and be able to regulate it.

PRACTICE:
STRETCH AND LISTEN

· Go somewhere quiet with room to stretch. Stand with your legs shoulder-width apart.

· Take a deep breath and allow your body to relax.

· Lift your arms straight up and reach as high as you can. Hold them up for five seconds and bring them back down. Repeat five times.

· As you stretch, listen to your thoughts. What are you thinking about? After you're done with the exercise, reflect on why you may have had those thoughts.

SPEAKING TRUTH

"Just because you want something to happen doesn't mean it's going to."

—KANAN JARRUS

PRACTICE:
FREE WRITING

· Grab pen and paper. Set a timer for fifteen minutes.

· Take three deep breaths. For fifteen minutes, write whatever comes to your mind. Don't stop to correct spelling or punctuation. Let your fears, anxieties, hopes, and everything else spill out. Write about how you're feeling, your wildest dreams, or literal dreams you have had while sleeping. Anything. Try to dig under the superficial layer, but keep your pen moving. The most important thing is to keep the words flowing, rather than overthink what you're writing.

· Repeat this practice at least three times a week. You will find you have cleared some head space, and you may be surprised by your insights.

Kanan's Padawan Ezra Bridger has much to learn, not only about the Force, but about the galaxy and life. Kanan often has to share harsh realities with Ezra—including this version of reminding Ezra that life isn't fair.

Writing down our desires will not make them come true, but words do have power. Getting emotions and thoughts out of our heads can provide clarity and unclutter the mind. One way to learn new things about ourselves can be by committing thoughts to paper.

FOR ANGER

"A challenge lifelong it is, not to bend fear into anger."

—YODA

The most centered, intelligent person you can think of has fears and flaws. Even Yoda. The Jedi master shares with Ezra Bridger the perhaps surprising news that even he was consumed by fear during the Clone Wars. Those who wield the Force must be especially cautious of fear, which can lead someone down a path to anger, and so to the dark side.

Anger is an especially powerful emotion, and the Jedi are right to give it a special focus of attention.

It can be a challenge to prevent anger from taking hold. It's an explosive emotion that hits quickly. Without consideration, the mind can respond reactively, essentially throwing fuel on the fire. However, if we reframe the mind to view anger as what it is—an energy that comes and goes—we can let it in and then say goodbye, without inviting it in to stay and take root.

PRACTICE:
ANGER REFLECTION

- Sit in a comfortable, upright position and close your eyes. Center on your breathing, in and out.
- Remember the last time you felt anger. What happened? How did your body react? If thinking about the episode causes the same heated response now, take deep, slow breaths.
- Observe the emotion of anger impartially. Recognize that it is a completely normal emotion, but also not one that needs to have power over you. Observe it from this cooler distance and with understanding, without getting caught in its charged current.

LISTEN

"Trust the Force."

—LYRA ERSO

PRACTICE:

MINDFUL MUSIC

- Select a piece of music or a song you have never heard before.
- Sit comfortably with your feet flat on the ground in a quiet place where you won't be disturbed. Put headphones on if they'll help you totally commit to the activity.
- Press play and actively listen to the music. Pay attention to the beats, the melody, the rhythm, the repetitions, and the movement. Identify specific instruments. How do the elements form the music, and how does the music make you respond?
- Try the practice again with music you know, or think you know, inside out.

One does not have to wield the Force to believe in its power. Lyra Erso believes in the Force and how it guides her, a faith she tries to pass on to her daughter, Jyn, in a troubling time.

Developing and trusting our powers of perception as a practice—trusting what we see, smell, feel, and hear—can help build trust in ourselves. We can sharpen our hearing by engaging in more mindful listening—to others (see page 27) and to music. How often do we actively listen to music without treating it as background?

COUNT ON NOTHING.

ONLY CHANGE.

—QUI-GON JINN

FOR STRESS

"I fear nothing. All is as the Force wills it."

—CHIRRUT ÎMWE

Though he's not a Jedi, Chirrut shares their deep beliefs, and their trust in the Force. He accepts what he cannot change and fights for what he can. And he knows the Force will guide him to the right outcome. Teased for his conviction by his friend Baze, he stays true to himself, and he is not afraid.

Remaining true to ourselves means digging under the surface. We need to recognize all aspects of our behavior and personality, even the ones we may not like. Stress can induce a number of unwelcome reactions, but we can learn to see those reactions coming.

PRACTICE:
STRESS MANAGEMENT

· When a stressful event occurs, pause to take deep breaths, and take note of how your body is reacting to the situation. Perhaps your heart is pounding or your shoulders have tensed. Acute stress can trigger your body's fight, flight, or freeze response. Pay attention to how it's doing so.

· Once you've become mindful of these symptoms, listen to your body when it starts reacting the same way. You may not be able to change the stressful situation, but recognizing the symptoms can help cue you to change how you react to it. The breathing exercise on page 79 can help your body reset.

BE HERE NOW

"Remember, concentrate on the moment.
Feel, don't think. Use your instincts." —QUI-GON JINN

Before young Anakin ignites his podracer's engines, about to face danger in a race few humans are capable of participating in, Jedi Master Qui-Gon Jinn offers guidance to center Anakin's mind. He cautions Anakin to be present in the moment—important advice because, in a podrace, distraction and overthinking can lead to a fiery crash.

Life is richer when we make an effort to be aware of what is around us, and how we relate to those surroundings in the moment.

PRACTICE:
SAVORING

- Choose an activity you do every day— maybe it's drinking coffee or walking to a bus stop. It can be something that takes just a few minutes.

- Use your senses to savor the activity. Think about each sip of coffee as a physical experience; notice its heat, aroma, and flavor. Tune in to the sounds and sights while you stroll. Any activity, no matter how seemingly mundane, can be enlivened and activated by paying it careful attention and noticing everything you can about it. You are here.

GRATITUDE

"When I was out there, alone, all I had was your training and the lessons you taught me, and because of you, I did survive. And not only that, I was able to lead others to survive as well."

—AHSOKA TANO

Jedi Masters train their Padawans in what they know about the Force—lightsaber technique and the ways of the Jedi and the galaxy—but also embody personal lessons in judgment, inner strength, responsibility, and much more. Ahsoka expresses gratitude to Anakin many times for his teachings.

Expressing gratitude is a form of recognizing gifts that we may have been granted but may not have recognized as such if we had not paused to give thanks. Capturing the things and people we are thankful for in a list can contribute to a more positive, more mindful mindset. To appreciate something is to notice it happened, and that can assist us in recognizing more opportunities to say "thank you."

PRACTICE:
GRATITUDE JOURNAL

- Select any blank notebook as your gratitude journal.
- Either just after you wake or right before bed, write down the date and at least three things or people you are grateful to have in your life, and write a sentence (or two) about why they make you feel this way. Your gratitude can be for something big or small.
- Occasionally look back through the journal and notice how much you have to be grateful for. Have you thanked the people you recorded in its pages?

CONNECTION

"May the Force of others be with you."

—CHIRRUT ÎMWE

PRACTICE:
NONJUDGMENTAL AWARENESS

- Mental chatter fills the mind. Whether you like or dislike something in yourself or others fuels part of that chatter. Next time you're people-watching, observe how often judgments come to mind.

- Judgments are thoughts. Acknowledge you are having the thoughts, then let them float away, without any weight or embellishment. Be—or strive to be—impartial, especially concerning self-judgments. As you become more aware of the judgments you make, they'll be less likely to preoccupy your mind.

While sitting on the streets of Jedha City, hoping for credits, Chirrut sends wishes of good will to those who pass by. With this short phrase of blessing and with the spirit of community, he connects himself and those around him in a positive light through the Force.

A positive spirit of mind can be difficult amid the inner monologue echoing in our heads—a monologue often full of judgments and critical evaluations, of ourselves and others.

CONNECT MIND AND BODY

"A strong belief can be more powerful than any army."

—AAYLA SECURA

Military might is not the only way to prevail in conflict. When a more underdeveloped civilization faces an incursion during the Clone Wars, Jedi Master Aayla Secura explains the power of belief to Ahsoka. That civilization also follows pacifism; they decline to help the Jedi defend their home. Their convictions are stronger than a lightsaber.

Believing in our bodies from the inside out increases our strength, which doesn't come from a single source. One way to align what's happening inside and outside our bodies is to focus on the blind spots we ignore.

PRACTICE:
ROLL OUT TENSION

· Get massage therapy balls—they shouldn't be too firm or too soft. Or try a firm, medium orange.

· Lie down in a relaxed position. Take three deep breaths, inhaling and exhaling slowly, to center yourself. Close your eyes.

· Spread your awareness to your body, noting anywhere you're holding tension—for instance, the bottom of your feet or your shoulders.

· Open your eyes and gently massage those areas using the therapy balls. Attending to these spots means you'll forge stronger communication between your mind and your body.

SEE THE BIGGER PICTURE

"Luminous beings are we, not this crude matter. You must feel the Force around you; here, between you, me, the tree, the rock, everywhere, yes."

—YODA

PRACTICE:
FOREST BATHING

- Find a nearby green space. It doesn't have to be a literal forest, just somewhere that you feel surrounded by nature, with space to wander.
- Choose a flat trail or an area to explore.
- Walk slowly, observe, and experience the area. Open your senses. Breathe, slowly and deeply. See how sunlight filters through the trees. Listen to the sounds, the calls of creatures and insects, and the rustling of leaves. Sit beneath a tree and feel the bark against your back. Bathe yourself in its peace.

Luke is skeptical of the powers of the Force despite Yoda's teachings. The wizened Jedi Master tries to reset Luke's cynicism by pointing out how the Force's radiance cascades through the galaxy and shapes life. He knows that Luke would see past the limitations he's imposing upon the Force, he could better wield its energy.

When we lose sight of the bigger picture, Yoda's words can serve as useful guideposts. We can ground ourselves in the ebb and flow of this world by immersing ourselves in nature.

OBSERVATION

"If this is the path you're called to, then this is the path you must follow."

—OBI-WAN KENOBI

PRACTICE:
SENSES JOURNAL

· Get a notebook, ideally one dedicated to this purpose, and a pen.

· Sometime before bed, write a journal entry about your day, but only from your senses' perspective. Try to record three to five (or more) items for each sense—seeing, hearing, tasting, touching, smelling. Repeat daily.

· Recording these experiences in the journal will make you more likely to notice—and appreciate—what you're sensing as it happens.

The Jedi Council extends an invitation to Qui-Gon, but because the Jedi Master knows himself, he declines. He realizes joining the Council does not align with his goals. Obi-Wan supports his master's decision; his teacher listened to his heart, and maybe the Force.

It can be invaluable and informative to take a moment and think about how we can listen to our heart—how to better recognize our place in the context of the world and our own path. Experiencing everything as fully as possible is a step toward that goal. The more we notice about the world, the more we notice about ourselves.

AWAKENING

"Rey, never be afraid of who you are."

—LEIA ORGANA

While Rey trains her mind and body to harmonize with the Force, she confronts dark doubts within. Leia offers Rey this expression of acceptance to help her leave her past behind.

Our family names and the legacies that come with them do not define us, but we should not be afraid of who we are, either. We can make this decision every morning, and give ourselves a boost to start the day by being truly awake and aware. This moment of mindfulness will set the tone for the day ahead and keep us close to our thoughts—especially the ones we have about ourselves.

PRACTICE:

MEASURED BREATHING

- Before you get out of bed, give yourself a quiet moment.
- Sit on the edge of your bed with a straight back. Take a deep breath from your belly through your nose, silently counting to three as you inhale. Hold the breath as you silently count to five. Exhale forcefully through your mouth while you count to six.
- Repeat three to five times.

ACCEPTANCE

"Only you can change yourself."

—BENDU

The Force—sensitive Bendu calls out to Kanan Jarrus as he is meditating, the Jedi Knight having been blinded in battle by Darth Maul. When the two meet again, Bendu, who stands between the light and the dark, offers the wisdom that external forces do not make someone good or evil; that power lies only within one's self.

Instead of investing energy in conditions we cannot change, we must strive to accept those conditions as they are. Accept that sometimes situations are already established, and all we can do is react to them. Think about yourself, all your attributes and behaviors, and practice self-acceptance.

PRACTICE:
SELF-ACCEPTANCE MEDITATION

- Sit with your back straight but relaxed, in a comfortable position. Close your eyes.
- Take three deep breaths, inhaling slowly through the nose and out through the mouth. Then breathe naturally.
- When your mind wanders—and it will—repeat this mantra softly, or in your head: "I am doing enough. I have enough. I am enough."

LEARN TO FLOAT

"I know what I have to do, but I don't know if I have the strength to do it."

—BEN SOLO

PRACTICE:
RIDE THE WAVE

· When you feel a strong emotion, positive or negative, observe everything about it. How did your body react? Did your mind linger on the emotion?

· The next time you feel that emotion, focus on your breath. Imagine the emotion as a wave you are riding to the shore. Every wave that begins will end. Once it does, you can paddle back out into the surf, ready for the next wave.

After an epic lightsaber battle, and a life-changing moment of healing by Rey, Ben Solo sees the image of his father, Han. The moment mirrors their last encounter on Starkiller Base, but with a very different outcome. This time, young Solo is able to embrace his role as son and push himself away from the dark side, throwing his lightsaber into the waves. He chooses the light.

Mindfulness enables those who practice it to survive waves of change or emotion. As the founder of integral yoga, Swami Satchidananda, taught, "You can't stop the waves, but you can learn to surf." With awareness and patience, we can control how our mind and body react. Understanding that life will be an unending cycle of waves is the key to helping us stay above them.

IN A DARK PLACE,

WE FIND OURSELVES,

AND A LITTLE

MORE KNOWLEDGE

LIGHTS OUR WAY.

—YODA

ACCEPT FAILURE

"The greatest teacher, failure is."

—YODA

Yoda continues to present lessons to Luke, even after the diminutive Jedi master has left his physical form. In this particular guidance, reflecting on Luke's apprentice, Ben Solo's, turn to the dark side and becoming Kylo Ren, Yoda presents a more expansive picture of the way Padawans and masters learn from one another.

No one enjoys failure, but everyone fails, and everyone is imperfect. Circumstances are also imperfect. We don't need to (figuratively) exile ourselves like Luke when we inevitably make mistakes. If we can teach ourselves not to let these imperfect moments drive our actions, we can feel more free.

PRACTICE:

ACCEPT IMPERFECTION MEDITATION

- Sit with a relaxed, but straight, back in a comfortable position with your feet flat on the floor. Close your eyes.

- Focus on your breath, inwardly saying "in" and "out" as you inhale and exhale.

- You may think you're doing it wrong or that you're bad at meditating because stray thoughts trickle in. You are doing great. We are all imperfect. Mentally repeat this mantra anytime you latch on to a self-judgmental thought: "I am imperfect, and that is okay."

FOCUS

"Keep your concentration here and now where it belongs."

—QUI-GON JINN

As a Padawan, Obi-Wan's mind always seems to be looking ahead–in part because Yoda has advised him to be mindful of the future. It is up to his Master, Qui-Gon, to draw Obi-Wan into the present. He reminds the young man not to focus on his anxieties, and while he doesn't contradict Master Yoda's counsel, he adds that one should not look to the future at the expense of that moment.

We can also heed Qui-Gon's advice. Digital buzzes, beeps, and other alerts are a mainstay of modern life. They and many other disturbances abound, and they take away from keeping our minds in the here and now. Some people are better at seeing past distraction than others, but even those who feel they have adapted to interruptions may find a pleasant difference in acting to curtail them.

PRACTICE:
DISTRACTION MANAGEMENT

- While working, observe and record how many distractions throw you off task. Reflect on the distractions at the end of the day: how many can you control?

- The next day, make changes to minimize those interferences. This can include turning off pop-up notifications, closing chat programs, and setting certain times to check email instead of opening messages the instant they land in your inbox. Make conscious choices rather than reactive ones about which distractions to allow.

FOR EMOTIONAL TIMES

"The Force brought me here. Brought me to Rey and Poe . . .
It's real. I wasn't sure then, but I am now."

—FINN

Finn has traveled to the oceanic moon of Kef Bir with his friends as the next step in their dangerous, planet-hopping mission to find and confront Emperor Palpatine. Describing their trajectory to fellow former stormtrooper Jannah, he makes this statement about the Force and its role in his life and journey. It's as though saying it out loud makes it real for him.

Finn is on to something. We think in words, concepts, and feelings, and saying something aloud can be a form of recognizing it, whether it is positive or negative. Naming an emotion can lead to gratitude for situations and people that bring positive feelings, and it can take away the power we may feel that negative emotions hold over us. In noticing our feelings we can choose to hold on to them, or to release them and send them on their way.

PRACTICE:
LABELING EMOTIONS

- Grab a pen and a piece of paper or a journal you can keep with you.
- Throughout the day, name any emotions you experience and record them on your paper. Write a sentence about what may have caused that emotion.
- Review your labeled emotions at the end of the day, and reflect. Which emotions are positive and worth lingering over in the moment, and which are candidates for just trying to get past or avoid?
- Repeat this exercise as needed until you can label an emotion as it's happening, and keep or dismiss.

OPEN YOUR MIND

"Rey, these are your first steps."

—OBI-WAN KENOBI

PRACTICE:
A BEGINNER'S MIND

· Look at the areas in which you live and work. Imagine you are seeing them for the first time.

· What do you notice first? Consider each object, how you use it, and whether it inspires you.

· Continue this practice until you've evaluated everything in the area you're observing.

· Repeat as needed to help you look at the world with fresh eyes.

As Rey seeks answers about her family, she stumbles upon a calling of sorts. She has her first vision through the Force, but she doesn't know what it means. Obi-Wan calls out to Rey as she's in distress, telling her she has taken her first steps . . . toward what, she doesn't know yet.

Treating every day as though taking first steps and experiencing the world with a "beginner's mind" is a long-held principle of mindfulness. Trying to forget what we think we know, and asking questions, can keep the mind learning as though we're a child, unfettered and curious. The more we think we are an expert on a subject, the less space we leave for different perspectives and information.

JOY

"Truly wonderful the mind of a child is."

—YODA

When Obi-Wan and Chief Librarian Jocasta Nu search the Jedi Archives for the planet Kamino and come up empty, they are lost. It takes going to a group of younglings to find the answer—younglings who are not stuck in their own set beliefs (e.g., that if something can't be found in the Archives, it does not exist). As Yoda observes, children's minds are uncluttered, free of adult burdens and the many preconceptions about the world. They can see possibilities those more closed-minded cannot.

Resetting our minds to a more curious state can be like removing a dam from a river or a stream. We can facilitate this.

PRACTICE:
ANIMAL OBSERVATION

· Look for an animal outdoors (a squirrel, a bird, or an insect).

· Follow it with your eyes. Pay attention to its movement and behavior, and note its color and characteristics. It's interesting, isn't it? Focus your attention on the animal and slow your breathing. If your mind wanders, refocus, and appreciate the calm from this undivided attention and connection with nature and another life.

STAY ON TRACK

"I need someone to show me my place in all of this."

—REY SKYWALKER

PRACTICE:
MINDFUL CHECK-IN

· Establish several times during the day to check in with yourself. You can schedule these during certain daily events (e.g., the dog's morning walk), or set alarms as reminders for when you know you can carve out five minutes.

· During each check-in, ask yourself: *What am I experiencing in this moment?* Consider emotions, moods, and thoughts at that time as well as over the course of the day. Are you acting according to your intentions—how you would like to be feeling? If not, what could you do to change this for the better?

Rey feels a little lost when she finds Luke in self-exile on the remote world of Ahch-To. She has traveled into the Unknown Regions to find clear answers about her role in the galaxy. But it is not so simple.

Our place in the galaxy, so far as we can define it by intention, is up to us. Regular check-ins with ourselves about our place and presence, here and now, can help foster the relationship between our mind and our goals. How can we pay attention to where we are going if we don't pause to consider where we are?

FEEL THE FORCE

FLOWING THROUGH YOU.

—MACE WINDU

LOOK INWARD

"Close your eyes. Feel it. The light.
It's always been there. It will guide you."

—MAZ KANATA

Rey visits Maz's castle in order to help deliver BB-8 to the Resistance, but while there, she opens a door to self-discovery. The Force reaches out to her and draws her to the Skywalker lightsaber stored beneath the castle. When touching it brings Rey a bewildering vision, Maz's counsel and comfort to Rey is that this light of the Force is a strength within her.

Like Rey, we have inner strength. The light is always present, though the pressures of life may sometimes dim its edges power or threaten to overshadow it. Feeling inner strength can come from turning our focus physically inward, and we can support this connection with an invigorating stretch.

PRACTICE:
A CENTERING STRETCH

- From a standing position, set your feet wide apart, past your shoulders, and lift your arms so they are parallel to the floor, pointing right and left.

- Turn your left foot slightly to the left, and turn your right foot ninety degrees so it is parallel with your right arm. Bend your right knee so it is above your right ankle. Turn your head to the right.

- Close your eyes and hold the pose for fifteen to thirty seconds, inhaling slowly and deeply, focusing on the position of your body and the feeling of your breath. Repeat on your left side.

LOOK INSIDE

"Your eyes can deceive you. Don't trust them."

—OBI-WAN KENOBI

Thanks to the Force, Jedi have a sensory sensitivity, but as Obi-Wan trains Luke on Tatooine, he reminds him to avoid solely relying on sight. He implies that our eyes can send the mind incomplete or even incorrect information. Luke needs to be aware of everything, even if he can't see it.

In the case of mindfulness, observation is a useful tool— as all sensory experiences are. However, we do not need our eyes to see. By closing our eyes, we may note an aspect of our environment we have not "seen" before.

PRACTICE:

VISUALIZATION EXERCISE

- Sit or lie down on your back in a comfortable position. Close your eyes.
- Call to mind one of your favorite relaxing places—perhaps it's a mountain lake or a snow-covered cabin. Wherever you've chosen, imagine yourself there. Visualize each detail you can think of, the evergreen trees or a roaring fireplace. Now imagine the rich scent of those trees or the warmth emanating from the fire.
- Sink into this visualization for 15 minutes to unwind.

BRAINSTORMING

"There are questions, questions that need answering."

—AHSOKA TANO

PRACTICE:
MIND MAP

- On a large sheet of blank paper, write the main topic or problem you're working through in the middle, and draw a circle (or any other shape) around your words.

- In the area close to the center, note subtopics—other issues affecting the situation—by writing them in spaces adjacent to the central topic. Draw a shape around each of them, too, and draw lines connecting them to the central topic.

- Now explore concepts corresponding to each subtopic, noting related issues and aspects near each. Free associate, with a nonjudgmental mind. Raise new topics and explore further. Make connections by drawing lines. Be curious and open to what ideas arise.

When Force users have questions, they can turn to the Force for guidance. When Ahsoka's instincts tell her something is happening with her former master, Anakin, she employs meditation as one tool to find answers.

Brainstorming is a good way of finding answers, as well as discovering new questions. It can help in both presenting the bigger picture and amplifying an understanding of the details. Making a mind map can help us focus concentration on a task or a situation by using a visual system to classify information and stimulate the imagination. This method lets creativity in and organizes ideas in a way that can help them stick.

SIT TALL

*"You always have a choice to be better.
You always have a choice to pick the right path."*

—ASAJJ VENTRESS

Wisdom sometimes comes from unexpected sources. Asajj Ventress, a one-time dark side assassin, struggles with leaving darkness behind for a more moral direction. But she recognizes that it's never too late to change and shares this with Jedi Master Quinlan Vos.

Making better choices applies to matters big and small, including choices about how we sit. It may seem minor—although consider how often we are sitting—but being in tune with our posture is yet another practice to help us be more mindfully aware. Assessing our posture and repositioning means we'll improve it. It's something we can do any time we are sitting.

PRACTICE:
MINDFUL POSTURE

- Pay attention to your posture throughout the day. Are you slouching or contorting any part of your body while you sit? Does the position you're in require any effort? Note where your body makes contact with what you're sitting upon, and how those parts of your body feel.

- Now deliberately and gently readjust your body to straighten your spine. As you do so, see how your body reacts to the change. What do the new points of connection feel like? Does your seat adequately support a healthy posture?

- Regularly take a moment to review your posture and straighten, and you'll eventually do so automatically.

SEE WHAT IS THERE

"If you live long enough, you see the same eyes in different people."

—MAZ KANATA

Living for more than a thousand years affords Maz Kanata the chance to meet many beings. She is deeply observant, and has been alive long enough to see patterns—not only in the galaxy, but in those who pass through her castle and safe haven. She peers at Finn and sees something familiar.

How often do we really see what is in front of us, as opposed to what we assume to be true and familiar? By deliberately examining our surroundings, by focusing the mind and opening our eyes, we can be more present in the moment.

PRACTICE:
WINDOW SIGHTS

· Peer outside through a window in a familiar place. Start by looking closely at what is right in front of you, then slowly expand your vision farther and farther to the end of your sight line. Then return your gaze to where you began.

· Rather than itemize what you see, take in shapes, colors, patterns, and textures. How do your nearby observations change after you look into the distance?

· When finished, consider what you now notice about the surroundings that you did not notice before.

SKILL IS THE

CHILD OF PATIENCE.

—OBI-WAN KENOBI

WAITING

"I know it's hard, but you have to be patient."

—AHSOKA TANO

So many circumstances are uncontrollable, and being unable to take decisive action toward a resolution can be discouraging. When a young prince is despondent about something he can't change, Ahsoka advises patience.

Waiting is an inescapable part of life. When we wait, it's practically instinct to try to find some activity, any activity, to fill what feels like a hole in our time. We grab a book, play a game, scroll through our phones, listen to a podcast— *anything* to make waiting less boring. But if we are going to wait regardless, why not practice mindfulness? You'll never have the present moment again; try exploring it before you turn to distraction.

PRACTICE:
MINDFUL WAITING

- The next time you find yourself waiting on hold or in line, accept that you're waiting, and release any frustration or annoyance you feel.
- Stay aware while you wait. Take slow breaths. Check in with yourself. Practice a sensory exercise (see page 16). Use whatever amount of time you have to be present.

LISTEN TO YOUR BODY

*"Even a moment can be an eternity in the Force. Center yourself.
Quiet your mind, and you will hear the Force's will."*

—MACE WINDU

When Jedi connect to the Force, they tap into an energy field, created by all living things, which binds the galaxy together. And if, as Mace Windu says, a moment in this connection can be an eternity, imagine the vast amount of information available to them by being aware of it. But to do so, they must quiet their minds and be ready to listen.

Bringing conscious attention to the state of your body can be a crucial step for wellness and peace of mind. Doing this regularly can encourage forming a kinder, more in-touch relationship with our bodies. It's an exercise that will yield benefits whether conducted for a few minutes or a half hour.

PRACTICE:
BODY SCAN

· Lie down in a relaxed position. Take three deep breaths, inhaling and exhaling slowly, to center yourself. Close your eyes.

· Starting with your left foot, scan every part of your body—each toe, each joint—with your mind. The speed at which you scan depends on how much time you have, but the slower the better.

· As you scan, note any sensations you feel, without focusing on why you might feel them. You may also sense nothing more than your internal systems doing their thing. Note that, too.

· After you've scanned your body from your toes to your scalp, expand your awareness to your body as a whole. Focus on your breath, and gently open your eyes.

TAKE THE TIME

"Slow down, Anakin. A great leap forward often requires taking two steps back."

—OBI-WAN KENOBI

PRACTICE:

ONE TASK AT A TIME

- Make a list of your tasks for the week, personal or professional.
- Lay aside a set amount of time for each task, maybe a little less than you think you'll need.
- Focus completely on the task at hand. Turn off notifications. Close your email and social media apps. Disconnect from the internet if you can. Go all in on completing each task with as few interruptions as you can manage.

Urgent conditions often seem to require urgent reactions. But the best solution to a problem may mean pausing to get it right—something Obi-Wan explains to his Padawan, Anakin. It can be more important to be thoughtful than to be quick.

The modern workplace cultivates multitasking. And though, thankfully, this rarely rises to the level of an "emergency," it can affect how we rush through our days. Checking email while putting together a presentation and accepting calendar invites can be, all too often, the norm, even if it's counter-productive. By taking two steps back and planning to tackle one project at a time, we may find better ways of working and solutions we might not consider when our attention is divided.

THE GROUND BENEATH YOU

"The belonging you seek is not behind you. It is ahead."

—MAZ KANATA

The past shapes who we are, but it does not hold all the answers we need, as Maz tenderly counsels Rey following her unsettling visionary encounter with the Force on Takodana. Maz points Rey forward, toward her future and her destiny.

We can remind ourselves to look ahead with a walk—specifically, a walk that isn't about arriving at a destination. Being here, and now here, and now here, rather than getting *there* or getting in steps is the point of mindful walking: to bring your mind and body in sync.

PRACTICE:
WALKING MEDITATION

· Find somewhere you can walk about twenty paces back and forth, undisturbed. Keep your eyes open.

· Take three deep breaths. Then walk at a slower pace than usual, placing your focus on the way the soles of your feet connect with the ground. Go back to this rhythm whenever your mind wanders.

· Walk on the same path for at least ten minutes. While continuing the rhythm, pay attention to other aspects of your movement over the course of the meditation. How does lifting your right leg, or left, or the motion of your arms, affect other parts of your body? Feel consciously how your physical self and forward motion are connected.

FOR CALM

"You will know when you are calm, at peace. Passive."

—YODA

PRACTICE:
BREATHING FOCUS

· Concentrate on your breath. Close your eyes if it helps. Make a committed, conscious effort to bring yourself to the moment.

· Take one long, deep breath, then exhale at the same rate. As you inhale, note where you most feel the breath—your nostrils or your chest. Do the same when you exhale. Note these sensations in your mind, and follow them as you breathe.

· Continue focusing on your breath for at least thirty seconds.

When you are centered, your brain has more space to work. Yoda tells Luke he'll know the light side from the dark side when he is at peace. He'll feel the difference. Settling into a quiet space invites the clearness needed to see different perspectives as well as the middle ground. Luke does the opposite of this when he enters the cave on Dagobah. He worries so much about the dark side that he cannot feel the light.

Focusing on breath comes up in mindfulness practices again and again. It's something we can do and control. Bringing our full attention to our breathing brings the mind only to that singular action. This is useful whether already in a calm state, or if one needs to move into a more tranquil state . . . even if the stakes are not as high as distinguishing between the light side and the dark.

ACKNOWLEDGMENTS

I could not have written this book without the support and expertise of many others . . . and many deep, energizing breaths. I want to give special thanks to Dr. Andrea Letamendi for guidance, insight, enthusiasm, and support; and to Christy Black for helping me see the connection between the body and the mind in a new way. I would not have stumbled into the healing world of meditation without Miracle Laurie's guided group meditations at Hero's Journey Fitness in Los Angeles; forty-five minutes have never been so productive for my well-being. Thank you for opening the door. And I wouldn't have kept up with regular meditation if not for Marianne Virtuoso; thank you for introducing me to the Calm app and its many helpful tools.

I would also like to acknowledge and recommend these books and resources as helpful:

· *Full Catastrophe Living*, by Jon Kabat-Zinn, PhD
· *Mindfulness in Plain English*, by Bhante Gunaratana
· *The Little Book of Mindfulness*, by Patrizia Collard, PhD
· UCLA's Mindful Awareness Research Center (MARC) - https://www.uclahealth.org/marc/

I'm so pleased to have worked with my editor, Steve Mockus, at Chronicle Books again. Steve, thank you for leaning into this concept and being an Obi-Wan to my Luke. Thank you to Christina Chung for the absolutely perfect illustrations and collaboration. Thank you to Evelyn Furuta and Kim Di Santo for setting our work in a lovely, relaxing design. Thank you to Chronicle Books and Lucasfilm for the opportunity to dive in to the Force and how it relates to mindfulness in our everyday lives.

Finally, my unending gratitude to my husband, Aaron, for being my rock and the actual best.

ABOUT THE AUTHOR

Amy Ratcliffe is the author of *Star Wars: Women of the Galaxy*; the managing editor for *Nerdist*; a host; and an entertainment reporter featured at StarWars.com, *Star Wars Insider*, *IGN*, and more. She cohosts the *Lattes with Leia* podcast. Based in Los Angeles with her husband and two cats, she enjoys taking mindful walks and connecting with nature at Descanso Gardens.

ABOUT THE ILLUSTRATOR

Christina Chung is a Taiwanese-Hongkonger-American illustrator, raised between Seattle and Singapore and currently based in Brooklyn, New York. Her work focuses on intricacies, color and symbolism, drawing inspiration from the natural world and powerful storytelling. Her clients include Lucasfilm, the *New York Times*, the *Washington Post*, and NPR.